The City of
Once Upon a Time

*A Children's True Story of
Williamsburg in Virginia*

BY

GILCHRIST WARING

ILLUSTRATED BY

ELMO JONES

THE DIETZ PRESS, INCORPORATED
RICHMOND, VIRGINIA

INTRODUCTION

We introduce our friends to other friends because they are good and true — because we believe that benefit and enjoyment will result from their acquaintance.

For the same reason, writers of history often introduce the work of other writers of history — because they have confidence in them.

It is a pleasure to introduce Gilchrist Waring's book to you, young ladies and gentlemen, because it will be enjoyable and helpful — because it is good and true.

RUTHERFOORD GOODWIN.

Williamsburg,
Virginia

Down in Virginia there is a little old-fashioned city called Williamsburg. It stands on the ridge of the peninsula that separates the James and York rivers.

Long ago, when our country was very young, Williamsburg was Virginia's capital. At important times, people gathered there from every part of the colony. There were those who came to help the royal governor make the laws, and those who came on private business. Still, others came just for fun and merriment. Inns and taverns overflowed. Merchants put out their finest wares. And up and down the streets rolled handsome coaches, drawn sometimes by as many as six splendid horses.

THIS is a story about Williamsburg when she was Virginia's capital. The story begins more than three hundred years ago when North America was still a vast wilderness, the home of wild animals and savage Indians.

Part of this wilderness, called Virginia, was claimed by the country of England. And across the Atlantic, in tiny ships, came adventurous Englishmen to build homes and settle in Virginia.

The first adventurers built a village and fort on the north bank of the James River. They named the village Jamestown in honor of their king. And Jamestown, which was founded in the year 1607, was England's first permanent settlement in America.

MANY hardships came to our brave settlers. One of the worst was bitter warfare with the Indians. The Indians, fearful of losing their wilderness homes to the English, would hide behind trees and bushes and shoot deadly arrows at the colonists. At sight of the savages, the colonists would rush into the fort for protection. Then, from the shelter of the fort, they would fire their guns and kill many of the painted Indians.

As the years went by, more and more colonists came to Virginia to live. Many brought their wives and children with them. Some of the new colonists built homes in Jamestown, while others pushed on into the forest.

Sometimes the Indians were friendly. Sometimes their anger would flare up anew. Then bitter warfare would start all over again.

AT last the colonists thought of a plan to protect themselves from the Indians. Using pointed logs, they built across the peninsula tall fences called palisades. "We shall guard them carefully," they said, "and the Indians will find it difficult to harm the people that live within the palisades."

Behind the palisades some of the colonists built homes, and their settlement, which was called Middle Plantation, stood where Williamsburg stands today. So, palisades, to keep out the Indians, were the very beginning of the little city of Williamsburg.

THE first adventurers who came to Virginia hoped to find gold and precious stones. But there were none to be found. They learned, however, to raise tobacco and it brought them great wealth. From the Indians they had learned how to smoke. The people in England had learned to smoke too. They enjoyed the habit and were willing to buy as much tobacco as the colonists would raise and send to them. So tobacco became almost as valuable as gold and precious stones.

LATER, many Virginians lived on big tobacco plantations. Some of the tobacco planters became wealthy. They built beautiful homes, much like the homes in England. And Negroes were brought from Africa to work as slaves on the plantations.

ONE day a dreadful calamity came to Jamestown. The State House, where the men met to help make the laws for the colony, caught fire and was destroyed. Then Governor Nicholson said, "We should move our capitol to Middle Plantation. It is more in the center of the colony. The ground is higher there, the climate healthier." The people agreed. The capitol was moved. And in honor of King William the Third, who at that time ruled England, its name was changed to Williamsburg.

NEARLY two hundred and fifty years ago, when the capital was moved, the colonists did not find Williamsburg as it looks today. Along a crooked old horse trail stood only a few houses, a few stores, little Bruton Parish Church, and the College of William and Mary.

The colonists went right to work, changing the little frontier village into a capital. The crooked old horse trail was straightened and made into a wide, beautiful street. Little Bruton Parish Church, which was almost in ruins, was rebuilt. Today it stands in Williamsburg just as it stood more than two hundred years ago.

The home which was built for the royal governor was so elegant the people called it a Palace. In the market square was built a Powder Magazine, where arms and ammunition were stored to be on hand if trouble came.

NEAR the Capitol stood the Prison. Its cells were small and dark, its windows heavily barred. The worst criminals were shackled with leg irons and handcuffs. In front of the Prison stood the stocks and pillory. An offender was sometimes punished by being fastened in the stocks or pillory, where passers-by could stare at him and jeer.

ON Sunday nearly everyone went to Bruton Parish Church. The women and girls wore their prettiest frocks. The men and boys dressed themselves in their most handsome outfits. And when the governor drove up in his royal coach, everyone bowed and stared in admiration!

MANY young men and boys came to Williamsburg to attend the College of William and Mary. Some of the students later became brave colonial leaders. Others became great presidents.

The people who lived in Williamsburg built lovely homes surrounded by pretty grounds and gardens. Some of the flowers and shrubbery were brought all the way from England.

SHIPS from England brought to the colonists many things they wanted or needed. And what a day of excitement when a laden ship would appear! Eager hands would open boxes filled with firearms, furniture, clothing, and toys for the children. Dolls, dressed in the latest English styles, would be sent to serve as fashion plates for the women.

IN old Williamsburg the people used candles for lights. They drew water in buckets from deep wells and cooked their food over open fireplaces or in Dutch ovens.

Postriders carried the mail. Sometimes it took weeks for a letter to reach a distant friend. Journeys were made in boats, in coaches, or on horseback.

As the girls in old Williamsburg grew up, they learned to sew and do fancy needlework. When they walked in the sun they wore bonnets and long gloves to prevent freckles and sun tan.

There was a longing in every boy's heart to be an excellent horseman. No sports were more keenly enjoyed by the colonists than horse racing and fox hunting.

Nearly everyone, young and old, knew how to dance. And great celebrations were made lively with the ringing of bells, the roar of cannon, bonfires, and magnificent fireworks.

THE House of Burgesses met in the Capitol in Williamsburg, usually in the Spring and Fall. The members of the House of Burgesses were men selected by the Virginia colonists to help the royal governor make the laws.

These were times of fun and frolic, as well as of serious business. And from near and far, the plantation people poured into Williamsburg. There was barely room for all. Fairs were held. There were fireworks, horse racing, contests, and cock fights. Sometimes the governor gave an elegant ball. Those invited considered themselves highly honored. Others might dance at home or in taverns, or amuse themselves by attending Williamsburg's theatre, the first to be built in England's American colonies.

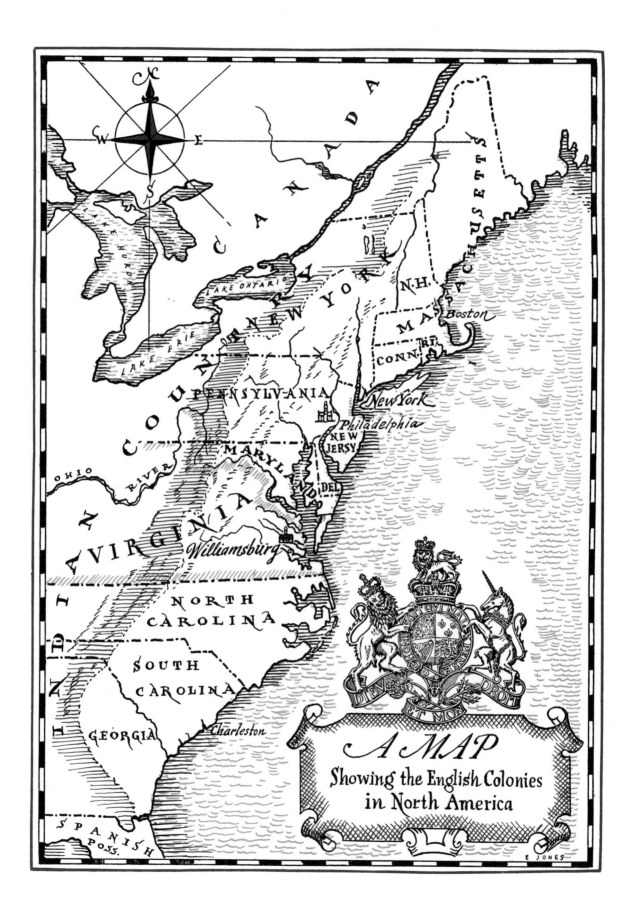

A MAP

Showing the English Colonies
in North America

VIRGINIA was now no longer England's only American colony. Many people who had come from England to settle in the New World had selected other landing spots along the Atlantic coast. And the big wilderness, which in the beginning had been called Virginia, gradually became divided into thirteen separate colonies. Each colony had taken a name of her own and had her own capital.

As time went on, the Virginia colony began to grow up. She became strong and powerful. However, across the Atlantic, King George the Third, at that time England's ruler, did not understand his grown-up colony. He did many things that made the people angry and unhappy.

"You may help make some of your laws," he said, "but there are some I shall make for you."

The colonists thought this very unfair indeed. They felt they had a right to help make all their own laws. But King George the Third was a stubborn king. He did not care one whit what the colonists thought. Right or wrong, he intended to force them to obey!

THE people in Virginia's twelve sister colonies were also angry and unhappy about the shameful way King George the Third was treating them. Women whispered about it behind their pretty fans. At home, in the shops, at church, and on the streets, men talked about it amongst themselves. But, in all the thirteen colonies, no one dared openly to accuse the king of doing wrong. "If we disobey," they said, "the king will send his powerful army and navy to wage war on us." The colonists had no navy. They had only a few poorly trained soldiers.

ONE day there came to Williamsburg a young man who was to be a new member of the House of Burgesses. His name was Patrick Henry. He wore a faded, old coat and leather knee breeches. His wig was not powdered. Some of the members wore powdered wigs tied with silk bows, bright colored coats, gay silk waistcoats, and buckled shoes. The new member looked, indeed, as if he did not belong in the beautiful Capitol.

When Patrick Henry rose to speak, however, the elegant members soon forgot his shabby clothes. The words he spoke amazed them. Brave and tall he stood as he shouted that King George the Third was doing wrong!

PATRICK HENRY'S daring speech frightened some
of the members of the House of Burgesses.

"I am glad they are frightened," thought Henry.
"It is time we wake up and defy the stubborn king!"

Some of the members tried to stop the speech.
In reply, Patrick Henry threw back his head and,
louder than before, shouted his words of angry
defiance!

PATRICK HENRY'S speech gave the people added courage. And, as the years passed, colonists everywhere began openly to defy the king.

Patrick Henry felt that if the king continued to rule the colonists in an unfair manner, they would soon be little more than slaves. Once, in St. John's Church in Richmond, he stirred the hearts of all who heard him when, in one of his great speeches, he cried, "I care not what course others may take, but, as for me, give me liberty or give me death!"

Most people agreed with Patrick Henry. Many, however, remained loyal to the king.

AT last King George the Third completely lost his temper. Then he sent soldiers and ships to America to subdue the colonists. "They shall soon learn," he thought, "that, whether they like it or not, they must obey me!"

The first troops landed in the colony of Massachusetts. At sight of them the colonists were very angry, indeed, and became determined at once to fight the British Redcoats.

In Williamsburg Governor Dunmore had the ammunition taken from the Powder Magazine and stored on a British ship that lay in a nearby harbor. And when the Virginia colonists heard of this unfair act, they soon forced Governor Dunmore to pay for the stolen gunpowder. The Governor was now in terror of his life. So one morning, just at dawn, he and his family slipped out of the Palace and took refuge on the ship that contained the stolen gunpowder. They soon set sail and from that day until this Virginia has had no more royal governors!

THE war for freedom had now begun and a Commander in Chief must be appointed to lead the army. When news came that George Washington, a Virginian, had been selected, the people in Williamsburg were filled with pride. Washington had been an officer in the Virginia Militia and for many years a member of the House of Burgesses. He was brave and courageous. The people felt that he would surely lead the troops to victory and the colonists to freedom.

The first colony to form her own government, independent of England, was Virginia. Then, rejoicing, the Virginia people said, "Now we may select our own governor." And the first governor selected was none other than Patrick Henry. As much as the people loved Patrick Henry, some feared he was not elegant enough to live in the Governor's Palace. But what a happy surprise when he appeared dressed in a handsome black suit, a scarlet coat, and a wig quite as large, indeed, as any in the whole country!

WHILE the new and independant government of Virginia was being formed in Williamsburg, there were a few wise men from each colony meeting in Philadelphia, a city in Pennsylvania. There, with Virginia men leading the way, all agreed to join together in one strong body and declare the independence of all the thirteen colonies.

Now a very wise person must be chosen to write the Declaration of Independence and Thomas Jefferson was selected for the task. Thomas Jefferson, who was a Virginian, had attended the College of William and Mary and had been a member of the House of Burgesses.

THE signing of the Declaration of Independence, in Philadelphia, was followed by great rejoicing. Bells were rung! Fireworks were set off! People laughed and wept with joy!

The war, however, was still to be won. And the war was long and bitter. England's soldiers were better trained, better dressed, and had more supplies than our soldiers. George Washington often became discouraged. But he spoke words of cheer to his men and prayed for strength to win the war.

Lafayette, a young and brave French general, came to America to help the colonists. Later French troops and ships arrived. George Washington was overcome with joy. "With this new help," he thought, "Victory can surely be won!"

WHILE the war for freedom was being fought, Thomas Jefferson was made Governor of Virginia. Then he and the men who helped make the laws decided to have the capital moved from Williamsburg to Richmond.

The moving of the capital made the Williamsburg people sad. They did not have long, however, to think of their sadness. British troops soon moved into Virginia and, for a few days, Williamsburg itself was over-run and plundered by the enemy.

LATER, Washington and the French came to fight the British at Yorktown, a small town on the nearby York River. As the battle raged, our wounded soldiers were carried to Williamsburg. The College of William and Mary was used as a hospital for the French wounded, while Washington's wounded were taken to the Palace. And sad to say, the Palace was mysteriously burned while it was being used as a hospital for our wounded.

IN the meantime, the British in Yorktown were forced to surrender. Then the people went wild with joy. Again bells were rung. Fireworks were set off. And prayers of thanks were offered for the glorious victory. Later, a peace treaty was signed by the thirteen states and England. By signing the treaty, England acknowledged that we had won the war and gained our freedom.

DURING this time most of the defeated British soldiers had sailed back to England. The French who had so kindly helped us, had sailed back to France. Home again had gone our own soldiers, tired and weary but happy that the war for freedom was ended.

Now a constitution was adopted and a new government formed, which bound all the thirteen states into one great union. And George Washington, whom the people had learned to love so dearly, was chosen the first president to head our new nation.

AFTER the war for freedom was won, Williamsburg became a quiet country town. The beautiful Capitol, where the House of Burgesses had met, fell into ruins. Then it was burned and weeds grew over and around its foundations. Lovely old homes became older and older. Walls crumbled in. At last, many completely tumbled down.

FOR nearly one hundred and fifty years Williamsburg remained a sleepy little town. And as she quietly rested from her labors, our country grew from thirteen states into forty-eight states. We became a mighty nation, stretching proudly from the Atlantic to the Pacific.

ONE day not many years ago there came to Bruton Parish Church in Williamsburg, a new rector. His name was William A. R. Goodwin. Mr. Goodwin was not only a rector but a great dreamer . As he walked along the streets he dreamed of the many brave colonists who had lived and died there. And as he dreamed, he began to wish that the little once-upon-a-time capital might be rebuilt to live again.

MR. GOODWIN continued to dream and plan until at last there came to Williamsburg a friend, Mr. John D. Rockefeller, Jr., who listened carefully as Mr. Goodwin told his dream. Then Mr. Rockefeller said, "Mr. Goodwin, I will make your dream come true. Williamsburg, our little once-upon-a-time Virginia capital, shall be rebuilt to live again!"

THE work of rebuilding Williamsburg was soon begun and the dreamer's heart sang with happiness. Modern buildings were pulled down. Old buildings were restored. Buildings entirely destroyed were rebuilt on their old foundations. And before many years had passed, Williamsburg begun to look just as it had looked more than two hundred years ago.

TODAY, from every part of our country, people come to Virginia to see the little once-upon-a-time capital. Down the streets they walk, and through the old buildings. Their hearts are filled with happy pride as they think of the brave colonists who fought and died for our freedom. As they stand in the Capitol they remember Patrick Henry as he stood there long ago and shouted words of angry defiance at a stubborn English king. They think of George Washington, Thomas Jefferson, and the many others who struggled until freedom was won. As they walk along they think of the dreamer too. And they think of the kind, brave man who made the dreamer's dream of Williamsburg come true.